British Railway Diesel Memories

No. 86: D FOR DIESELS : 9

Norman Preedy

Copyright Book Law Publications 2015
ISBN 978-1-909625-49-5

INTRODUCTION

I was delighted to accept David Allen's invitation to compile a volume for the *D for Diesels* series using my own negatives. In doing so, I have tried to make an interesting and varied spread of pictures; both action and depot views are included and which were taken up and down the country. The coverage includes areas from all six regions of the old British Railways system when, unlike today, there were many different classes of locomotive at work. It made observing the trains and photographing them far more interesting.

All the images which appear in this album were captured on film cameras of medium and large format types mainly Rollieflex and Ensign Selfix models which gave the option of 12 and 8 exposures per 120 size film; you had to be very selective in what you took in those days. I used Ilford film all the time, either FP3 or FP4, which I processed myself.

I do hope that you the reader will gain as much pleasure from this album as I did putting it together. It certainly brought back many memories from a distant past.

Norman Preedy, Gloucester, June 2015.

(*Front cover*) **See page 48.**

(*Title page*) **'Pilot Scheme' EE Type 4 D207 speeds along the ECML near Carlton, Nottinghamshire, with an Up express for King's Cross on Saturday 8th August 1959.**

Printed and bound by The Amadeus Press, Cleckheaton, West Yorkshire
First published in the United Kingdom by Book Law Publications, 382 Carlton Hill, Nottingham, NG4 1JA

'Warship' D831 MONARCH runs along the seawall section of main line between Teignmouth and Dawlish in August 1961 with inter-regional cross country express 1N37 from either Plymouth or Paignton which was heading for Leeds, York or Newcastle. The Swindon-built B-B, which entered traffic on 11th January 1961, was allocated to Plymouth's Laira depot. Throughout its life D831 was only ever allocated to two depots, both in Devon – Laira and Newton Abbot – twice at the latter and three times at Plymouth during the time it was coded 83D and then 84A. Withdrawn on 8th October 1971, D831 spent its final months stored at Marsh Junction, Bristol but entered its birth place for cutting up in May 1972.

3

One of the later batch of EE Type 4s, and an LMR example too, D334 arrives at Bangor with the Up working of the *IRISH MAIL* during the summer of 1962. Only a year and a few months old – entering traffic 11th March 1961 – the Crewe North based diesel-electric is already showing signs of neglect with oil stains making their slow but inevitable progress down the body side of the big diesel.

'Warship' D600 ACTIVE (a lot of contradictions and irony concerning names plagued BR around this period) rounds the curve at Teignmouth in August 1961 with a Paddington bound express. Delivered from North British Locomotive Co. in Glasgow during January 1958, the big C-C was accepted at Swindon that same month and after all the necessary trials (and tribulations), was transferred to Laira depot during the following May. The Plymouth depot was to be D600's home throughout its short life which ended in December 1967 when it was condemned. It was one of the few diesel locomotives purchased by that perhaps most famous of scrapyards which was owned by the Woodham brothers at Barry. D600 was cut up there in March 1970; sister D601, formerly ARK ROYAL, survived in that same yard until June 1980 and was the last of the five to go.

EE Type 4 D201, working an inter-regional service from York to Bournemouth via Oxford, is passing Duckmanton South junction on the old Great Central main line on 22nd May 1959. D201 has yet to acquire any warning panels and looks fairly pristine for locomotive just over a year old. This particular working must have been part of the diagram which this Type 4 and its sisters worked from Hornsey depot during their formative years when they appeared to rarely rest between duties. BR intended to get their worth out of these locomotives and luckily for all concerned they lived up to the manufacturer's claims and hardly failed. D201 would probably come off this train at Leicester where a Western Region steam locomotive would take over for the trip to Oxford, where a Southern Region 'Light' Pacific would then take on the train to the south coast. Meanwhile, Duckmanton was situated in North Derbyshire amongst some of the most intensely mined land in Britain. Located four miles from Chesterfield, we are looking north at the overbridge carrying the Down ex-LD&ECR connection – which is going off on the left of the image – whilst the Up connection is coming in from the right behind the locomotive. The LD&EC main line was actually behind the camera. However, there is no sign of these railways today – or the coal mining – and this cutting now forms part of a woodland and nature reserve. For interested parties, the OS grid reference is SK448718. Watch out for the ghostly A3 which can thunder through at any time!

'Peak' Type 4 D5 CROSS FELL works a Liverpool train at speed near Weaver Junction in April 1961. All ten of the original 'Peaks' worked on the West Coast main line during their early days and were allocated between Camden, Carlisle Upperby, Crewe North, Edge Hill and Longsight depots at various times up to the early months of 1962 when they were all recalled to Derby, their train heating boilers removed, and then relegated to a life of working freight trains out of Toton yard to all corners of the BR network for the rest of their lives. Most of the ten went officially to Toton on 3rd March 1962 but our subject here became the first one to take up residence at what was then 18A, arriving on 24th February 1962. Sister D8 went to Nottingham shed on 10th February but then moved across to 18A shortly afterwards. Note that plain front ends were still the order of the day.

We've seen D200 at Stratford depot before but not actually inside the newly commissioned diesel depot. Here on Wednesday 11th June 1958 new meets new – well almost. Neither shed nor diesel locomotive were brand new but both had yet to be fully commissioned into their roles and everything was 'early days' so to speak. D200 had been here since March, and had already been joined by sisters D201 to D204. However, one of that number – D201 – had been seconded to Hornsey depot after arrival where driver training – in time for the GN main line services starting later in the year – was taking place. For those forthcoming GN services D206 to D209 were delivered new to Hornsey shed. In June 1959 the five GE Line engines – D200, and D202 to D205 – were transferred from Stratford to Norwich. Much has been written about these locomotives on the GE Line, some observers and indeed footplatemen have compared them to the Britannia Pacifics they replaced. Indeed some said they were no match for a 'Brit' in top notch condition!? We'll never really know I suppose. Meanwhile, the quiet and cleanliness of the shed is to be savoured before the engine is switched on and normality returns! Note the condition of our subject which can only be described as perfect!

A morning departure from Eastgate! On 4th February 1967 'Peak' D66 leaves Gloucester (Eastgate) with 1N70, the 1116 departure to Newcastle which will be worked right through by the Midland Lines based Type 4. In 1968 D66 and dozens of her sisters would be re-allocated to the Nottingham Division pool which was based on Toton maintenance. Such transfers were meant to bring standardisation to the maintenance procedures surrounding these locomotives but once again empire building was taking place within certain areas of BR. The motive power department of the former Midland Lines was being continually changed as were other areas of the former LM Region. As for the other regions!!!!! It certainly kept the enthusiasts on their toes but as for everyone who worked within BR it must have been a confusing business at times. No wonder the outfit never made a profit. Eastgate station has long since closed, and an ASDA supermarket now resides on the site. All rail transport at Gloucester is now concentrated on what was Central station.

9

North to Sheffield on what was essentially the same stretch of former Midland Railway but with a lot of miles in between the two centres. Another 'Peak' is awaiting its next turn of duty at Midland station on 20th June 1970. This is D32 which although sporting the newly acquired BR double-arrow logo, does also wear the 'D' prefix enabling its inclusion in this album. One day we'll probably get around to producing albums featuring diesels with the double-arrow and no prefix, and possibly with TOPS numbers too but that is somewhere in the future – the distant future! Note that the Type 4 has received full yellow ends by now to compliment the all over blue paint which was becoming the standard livery for the Seventies.'

In the wilds of the Cumberland fell country we see EE Type 4 D211 MAURETANIA heading the Down working of *THE MID-DAY SCOT* and approaching Shap summit whilst passing Shap Wells on 13th May 1966. The big diesel had been working these WCML expresses since being put into traffic in 1959 – the name was fitted on 20th September 1960 – but latterly it had been sharing the work with Brush Type 4s. It was of course about to get worse. A month earlier the old Western Division of the LM Region had changed the allocation system – just like the Midland Lines – from individual depots having batches of locomotives allocated to a general pooling arrangement, whereby all the main-line motive power was put into the Western Lines pool. It remained like that for just over a year when there was a quiet reversion to individual sheds again! D211 went to the Springs Branch depot on 2nd September 1967 by which time it was rarely working the crack express on the WCML or indeed any other line. Small Divisions for motive power purposes were created in June 1968, Wigan becoming part of the Liverpool Division, and then, less than a month later D211 was transferred to the Preston Division which stretched as far north as Carlisle! Meanwhile, this beautiful landscape was itself subject to massive change with the coming of the M6 motorway, and then the wires. However, before then another class of diesel was to make its debut on the WCML and we'll be meeting them forthwith.

11

With its No.2 end nearest the camera, EE Type 4 D401 rests at the Crewe North stabling point on 18th May 1969. Entering traffic during the week ending Saturday 9th December 1967, this was the second example of the class accepted by BR; D402 and D404 both followed during w.e. Saturday 23rd December 1967. For the record, D400 entered traffic during the week ending on the previous 7th October after months of testing. These fine looking machines were the culmination of the trials carried out some years beforehand by the 'Deltic lookalike' DP2 (see also *D for Diesels 5* which explains the tragic early demise of DP2) which did some superb work on the ECML but whose successors were chosen – ironically – to work expresses on the WCML! Considering it had been in traffic for almost eighteen months, the Co-Co is remarkably clean for the period. Both D400 and D401 came out of Vulcan Foundry partially fitted for multiple unit working (note the few jumper cables on the right side of the cab front) with positions for retro-fitting already cut and covered in the bodywork. The rest of the class came out with the 'cut and cover' but with no jumper cables or sockets fitted; internal wiring had however been made ready. The multiple-unit workings started in 1970 (all of the class had been through the works at Crewe during 1969 for the final jumper cable fitting) when the Anglo-Scottish expresses were accelerated ready for full electrification of the WCML in 1974. These 2,700 h.p. locomotives were coupled in pairs and worked between Crewe and Glasgow with one driver in charge of 5,400 horsepower – a big step on BR during that period. To say that they performed well would be an understatement but their complicated internal wiring and electronics required total dedicated maintenance which was to be lacking in later years. The dark patch half-way along the bodyside was not an oil stain it was a shadow from a yard lighting tower. Livery from new was all-over blue with numbers on both sides, and at both ends of the body; the BR double-arrow symbol was also generously applied to both sides of the cabs too. Sister D442 is stabled behind.

No messing about with the location of door handles on this class they all had two-position handles!

Such a common sight on the LM Region at this time, EE Type 4 D331 makes a stop at Birmingham (New Street) in August 1962. The front end has yet to acquire the small yellow warning panel. New Street is at present undergoing a rebuild and it would be quite difficult to match up this image with the present day scene.

13

D415 and sister D408 grace the SP at Crewe North on 28th June 1968. Although all were allocated to Crewe during their time on the LM Region, none of the class ever carried a shedplate but by the time they came into traffic, the cast metal plates were out of vogue; Crewe North shed didn't exist as a building; Crewe South shed was essentially closed, and the diesel depot to the west of the station never had need for little cast-iron plates with numbers on. The only plates visible on these particular locomotives were the cast rectangular plates with the usual builders' information – venue, year, number – and another informing the world that this class was actually leased to BR by an English Electric subsidiary company. Such was progress. Once deliveries of a class had commenced, it was normal practice for private manufacturers to release new locomotives to BR at regular intervals – English Electric had plenty of practice in that field – so that diesel locomotives could be accepted, tried, tested and then put into traffic at a planned rate. However, the Class 50s - as we shall call them from now on – arrived on BR property somewhat erratically. From D400s October 1967 appearance, nothing came out in November but December produced three examples from Vulcan Foundry; two in January; one in February then seven in March! From thereon until the holiday month of August the monthly totals were six, five, six, four, and two. September saw production lifted to four locomotives followed by five in October, three in November and finally D449 on the last day of 1968! Note how clean these locomotives were kept; I think something within the leasing agreement saw regular washing as set in concrete! We'll be seeing more of this class in forthcoming albums in this series.

14

NBL 'Warship' D603 *CONQUEST* waits to leave North Road station at Plymouth with the Up working of *THE CORNISH RIVIERA* on American Independence Day 1961. By now the big diesel-hydraulic was still not three years old but was looking much older although its ancient design features do nothing to enhance its looks. For diesel-hydraulics, the class tipped the scales on the somewhat heavy side weighing ten tons more than a 'Western' for instance. However, in the 'looks' department these 'Warships' and the 'Westerns' were aeons apart! Despite its rather short life, this locomotive and its four sisters made quite an impression on enthusiasts countrywide – it also made an impression on the WR Operating Department but that was of the wrong sort – but enthusiasts don't run the railway (admittedly, some do!). That Laira put the 'Warship' at the head of what was arguably the most important train coming out of Cornwall if not the West Country at that period must have been actioned' by a failure; the diesel is a something of a disgrace externally. Note the secondmans nameplate holder on the cabside just above the number – another motive power innovation which sank without trace. For those of you who never saw one of these, they were green with a cheat line.

15

From one disgrace to another but we have moved on in time, not to mention location. This is the lightweight version of the 'Warship' class – the 79-tons worth of B-B – and just like their larger brethren, they too had a somewhat curtailed existence. As can be gauged from the appearance of D806 CAMBRIAN externally no one gave them a second thought; Swindon and indeed WR authority in general appear to have given up. They couldn't get their own way and now they were virtually denying the existence of their creations. Strong words but truth be known, grown men can sulk with the best of children. The 'Warships' were living on borrowed time yet still putting in useful performances with some remarkable haulage feats in the right hands. The venue for this image is Exeter (St Davids) station on Thursday 9th July 1970 and D806 has just worked down from Central station with the stock it had earlier hauled from London's Waterloo station. In this image the B-B is wearing the remnants of the maroon livery once popular after Swindon overhauls. Already the first seven members of the class has been withdrawn but D806 itself was about to go into works for a major overhaul and repaint into an all-over BR blue livery; it survived until November 1972 by which time all the rest of the class had been condemned. Ironically, Plymouth, the home base for many of these locomotives was also a major Royal Naval dockyard (actually located in Devonport) used by a large element of Britain's Senior Service. In those days most, if not all, matelots travelling on leave or draft to some other naval establishment would travel by train, hauled in the main by one of these. I wonder what went through their minds when confronted by a filthy and neglected contraption such as this when it might be named after a ship they were serving on! PR never was a strong point for BR(WR).

Here is what was meant to be! The class leader D800 SIR BRIAN ROBERTSON inside Swindon works – looks like 'A' Shop – on 27th July 1958 displaying the fact that it was the first of its kind to be built at the Wiltshire plant and indeed by BR. Note that already a certain amount of road dirt has accumulated on the lower bodyside indicating that numerous test runs had already been conducted out on the main line although a trip to Paddington for the naming ceremony on 14th July would have rustled up some dirt en route. Like all publicity machines, the WR version made great store of the facts regarding the hydraulic motive power; I wonder how much publicity they gave BR's later decision to scrap the diesel-hydraulic principle. At this time only two of the North British large C-C 'Warships' had been delivered to BR and it would be towards the end of 1958 and into the first month of 1959 before the remaining three were put into traffic. D800 went to Laira in August and along with the two C-Cs took turns working the Up *CORNISH RIVIERA LIMITED*. That the Western Region did not have a good start with their chosen motive power is obvious but still they would not recognise the problems, especially in public – who does? Swindon-built D801 and D802 joined D800 at Laira by the end of the year. Of course, these three were of 2,000 h.p. only (despite what the legend on the publicity placard proclaimed) whereas the rest of the class ranged from 2,200 to 2,400 h.p. D800 didn't last as long in service as the majority of its sisters and was stored unserviceable in September 1968, withdrawal taking place during the week ending Saturday 5th October 1968. The beginning of the end for the class had begun! However, D801 had preceded them all when it was put into store at the end of June 1968 and then withdrawn during the first week of August! The finish off the early trio, D802 was also withdrawn during that week ending 5th October 1968. The cost of each of these locomotives in comparison to other main-line high-horsepower units was rather high but that's another story!

17

Images such as this do not normally make it into *DforD* because they are so modern but this illustration of Old Oak Common depot on 16th March 1974 is allowed because it has a 'D' diesel on display. Now we could be pedantic and say that the particular 'D' in question belonged to 'Western' 1055 WESTERN ADVOCATE which had its prefix painted over some years beforehand. However, the 'D' was still present at the front of the number and no matter how much paint was used to obliterate the casting it was always going to be there. Hence the inclusion – and I'm a 'Western' fan anyway! The diesel depot rose from the ashes of the former steam roundhouse sheds of which there were once four on the site, all joined under one roof. Rationalisation saw the roundhouses demolished (the empty space on the left contained the two northerly turntables), a new straight road servicing shed built (in the right background) and one of the original turntables, with its attendant stalls – all now outside – kept for stabling purposes. Alongside the 'Western' is an interloper from the LM Region which now carried its TOPS number 50004 (ex-D404) which had only just been renumbered. The Class 50 had done their job on the LMR and were now transferring to the Western Region to take over from the 'Westerns' which were being withdrawn as they were replaced! Naturally, the '50s' were not very popular amongst 'Western' fans but they were still coming, ready or not. From 1978 the Class 50s began to carry names, the names of British warships. It was about this time that maintenance and indeed external cleaning standards began to slip on the WR again. Haven't we been here before?

I make no apology for including another picture of a 'Western' Type 4. This image shows D1049 WESTERN MONARCH running alongside the sea wall stretch of railway between Dawlish and Teignmouth on 25th July 1974. A classic scene! The train, 1Z15, is an extra from Paddington to Plymouth.

The Brush Type 4s seemingly became the maids-of-all-work on BR from the mid-60s' but they were hardly given any special treatment by the motive power department. D1700's external appearance was typical of the class in general in this 24th September 1966 illustration captured at Basingstoke whilst the Co-Co was working the Bournemouth bound *PINES EXPRESS*. This Loughborough built locomotive had started life on the Western Region on 13th January 1964 at Old Oak Common depot but had transferred to Bristol's Bath Road depot a year later on 15th February 1965. From 23rd April 1966 it had been allocated to the LM Region's Western Lines, hence the W beneath the fleet number. Note though the oval stain on the lower section of the cab panel directly beneath that W where a cast shed plate had once been fixed. I wonder if it was one of the A82 examples featured on page 37 of DforD10? Note the super-elevation of the track at this point!

Brush D1925 stands in the yard at Gloucester Horton Road depot on 28th December 1965, just six days after being 'delivered' to Bath Road depot from Loughborough via Derby. Already the pristine finish is looking shabby with plenty of road dirt apparent but, it is winter. Compared with the Pannier over the other side of the yard D1925 does look immaculate! The chances are that the new Co-Co has been nowhere near Bristol yet and may still be on its delivery run, each depot at which it called using it on some small task or other. It was not unknown for such circumstances to prevail on all BR regions – one Doncaster-built BR Standard locomotive took seven weeks to reach its new home shed in Scotland after release from Doncaster Plant in the Fifties' – and the lack of an 82A or A82 shedplate strengthens that theory. The 'V' in the headcode signifies an inter-regional working to the Western Region, a freight, probably. During the period October to December 1966 this Brush along with sisters D1921-D1924, and D1926, were all transferred from the WR to Eastleigh on the Southern for a near two year stint to help out with heavy cross-country and Bournemouth-Waterloo workings beyond the capability of the BRC&W Type 3s. Of course they excelled themselves.

Another new one! D1961 had been completed at the Brush Loughborough factory in January 1968 but was not put into traffic. Instead the blue liveried Co-Co was sent to the Research Department at Derby RTC where it remained for the early months of 1968. On Sunday 5th May 1968 it was photographed in the works yard at Crewe having had a new piece of control gear fitted – the jumper cable of which can be seen above the right hand buffer – for electric train heating. Within days of this image being recorded, the locomotive was allocated to LM Western Lines. Except for the water staining from the roof drips and runs, the body is clean with no accumulated road dirt – its looks as though D1961 had done very little mileage and plenty of stabling in the open; but all that was to change. Alongside is another new piece of equipment recently delivered from the makers – EE Type 4 D423 which had arrived during the previous week with D422. The eagle-eyed amongst you will note the hinged side windscreens (also known as cinder screens in steam days) on the driver's side window of D423.

0-6-0DM shunter D2030 stables at March shed on 28th March 1965 after a recent visit (December last) to main works at Doncaster for a major overhaul. This particular example was one of the Swindon batch and was delivered to Cambridge shed on 28th October 1958. Within days it was whisked off to March shed during November and where it remained for the next six years, with a seven month break at Kings Lynn in 1960, before moving (on paper) to New England on 28th November 1964 (it was actually destined for works attention then). It appears that the New England residency was not taken up because here we are back at March. Moving to Ipswich in November 1965 (why, seemingly always November?). Surplus to requirements on the ER, D2030 was transferred to Eastleigh in May 1966 and then, in the following September, a final move took place which located the 0-6-0DM at Brighton. It was in Brighton where withdrawal took place during August 1969. Then came another move of no small mileage which took it to a scrapyard in Rotherham where, apparently, it was cut up in 1970 – November!

This is sister D.2012 brand new outside Swindon Stock shed on 16th February 1958. It was delivered to Cambridge depot on the 24th February (departed Swindon on 23rd) along with sisters D.2009, D.2010, and D.2011, the latter leading, our subject second in the cavalcade. Between December 1957 and July 1959 Swindon was responsible building forty-four of these useful locomotives for the Eastern Region and three for the Western. Next came another batch – D2114 to D2199 – for the WR, SR, NER and LMR which were built from July 1959 to June 1961. Finally D2370 to D2384 emerged from Swindon during the late summer and autumn of 1961. Meanwhile, Doncaster was building its share of the order with D2044 to D2085 produced from November 1958 to April 1959, D2089 to D2113 from April to December 1960, and D2385 to D2399 from March to September 1961. Now, compare some of the Doncaster built examples found in earlier *DforD* albums with these and then spot the differences to the exact same design produced by the two factories. Back to this image, note the number fonts in the previous image and this one are somewhat different; D2030 wears the Condensed Grotesque numbers – then BR Standard – applied at the recent visit to Doncaster whilst D.2012 has a sans serif style complete with the full point after the prefix (see also *DforD5* p.54). Note also the wrong facing BR crest which was still being applied during this period even though the College of Heralds insisted its use should cease! D2012 did better than its later sister and after gaining its TOPS number 03012 in February 1974 worked from March depot until withdrawn in December 1975. it was then sold to private industry and lasted until December 1990 when it was cut up in the yard of Mayer Parry in Snailwell. For an early view of D.2012 and her sisters at Kings Lynn, see *Dfor D4* page 48.

Its always nice to show something new or different and this image falls easy into the second category. This is Doncaster built D2398 which spent all of its short life working on the Southern Region as here at Branksome depot, Bournemouth on 2nd August 1970. Air-brake equipment had been fitted to the 0-6-0DM to enable it to shunt the SR air-braked passenger stock (indeed an air-braked stock); the rather prominent air tanks – one each side – do look like afterthoughts the way they have been located at the front of the cab. Besides the tanks, coupling hoses are set up on their own stands at opposing corners of the locomotive, and a cabinet has been provided on the front engine panel with easy access. A similarly fitted sister engine is buffered up on the right but once again detail differences can be easily detected. Note the top lamp iron over the radiator, one is a lazy 'S' type whilst the example on our subject is more like a corrupted 'T' on its side with the top stem set back. The lack of electrification warning panels is obvious too although the right hand shunter has one on display (there never was an equivalent warning panel for third-rail country which would seem to be a more likely source of danger). Bournemouth depot had about eight of this class allocated at the time when this image was recorded on film so we cannot second guess what the mystery engine was - my notes are not as clear as they could have been. D2398 had arrived on the SR at Hither Green on 30th September 1961, the penultimate example built at Doncaster, and it transferred to Weymouth on 28th May 1962, moving to Bournemouth on 30th March 1968. The air-brake equipment was probably fitted in time for the arrival of electrification of the Bournemouth line, and the onwards extension to Weymouth. In 1971 D2398 went to Weymouth for the summer season to help out on the boat trains on Weymouth Quay; for that work it was fitted with a warning bell and flashing light on the front face at the bottom of the radiator panel. Returning to Bournemouth after the cessation of the summer timetable, D2398 was withdrawn and then sold to Pounds Shipbreakers of Portsmouth, the actual cutting up being undertaken at Fratton. Was the flowerpot 'chimney' better than the traffic cone?

Another brand-new, just arrived, example of BR modernisation! NBL 0-4-0DH D2755 poses at Eastfield depot on 22nd May 1960. According to official records, this locomotive was allocated to Dalry road shed on 11th May 1960 but it obviously hadn't made the journey over to Edinburgh and was still undergoing acceptance trials in Glasgow. By now a modified radiator grill was being fitted to the new shunters as they came off the production line, the wire mesh giving way to this robust slatted design. The piping around the bufferbeams was a feature of these NBL shunters when they were delivered, a nice touch which was an echo of steam-era liveries. Perhaps that was the problem with NBL, they couldn't get out of steam locomotive thinking. Nevertheless these shunters were adequate enough, they did their job but the jobs themselves were becoming fewer. When D2755 eventually got to Dalry Road, it served at the former Caley shed until 24th October 1964 when it went to St Margarets. On 18th February 1967 it was transferred to Leith Central (the grandest diesel depot ever?) and from where it was withdrawn six months later on 3rd August 1967 during the mass cull inflicted on this class by the Scottish Region. Few went into private industry and all of them save a handful had been cut up by the end of 1968.

They became Class 01 under TOPS but only two of the original four (D2953 to D2956) Andrew Barclay 0-4-0DM survived long enough to receive the renumbering. D2956, photographed at Doncaster on 29th August 1967 was not one of the lucky? pair and was instead something of a misnomer in the fact that it was not even one of the original four from 1956 (*see also DforD2 page 52*). Up to July 1967 this particular Andrew Barclay 0-4-0DM had been in Departmental stock and numbered 81 in that fleet but when the original D2956 was withdrawn at Doncaster in May 1966, the four-coupled shunter was put into Running Stock and renumbered during July 1967. Note the very unorthodox font used for the letter and figures but note also the BR symbol – bang-up-to-date! The subject locomotive was actually withdrawn in November 1967 and then sold off to the British Steel Corporation at Briton Ferry. It didn't do much for the BSC and was cut up in August 1969. In this view the little shunter is working amongst acres of the Civil Engineers yard at Doncaster, with cranes and sludge carriers in attendance too.

Crewe-built 350 h.p. 0-6-0DE D3920 rests at Stratford, east London on Saturday 11th July 1970. Some ten years old by now, this locomotive had been around since its delivery to Greenock Ladyburn on 30th December 1960 (it was amongst the last batch of shunters produced at Crewe and was technically the penultimate example turned-out); how nice that Crewe managed to put D3921 (their last) into traffic before 1960 was out! Before D3920 arrived at Stratford on 23rd September 1968, it had spent four months at Tinsley after Polmadie dispensed with its services after just three months. The six-coupled shunter had transferred to 66A from 66D at the end of February 1968. In this image, the BR crest seems to have disappeared from its original location on the battery box, perhaps accumulated filth has obliterated the insignia but it didn't really matter by this time when the double-arrow symbol was being applied anyway. Note the TOPS panel beneath the fleet number but more importantly that 'D' surviving into another year. Unlike the renumbering into TOPS, we have very little record of when the prefix was taken off (painted out) but it took place over a number of years and some lasted a surprisingly long time after they should have been eliminated. Our subject went on to become 08752 in March 1974.

(*above and below*) Ex-works in their new blue livery and BR double-arrow symbols, 350 h.p. 0-6-0DE shunters D3993 and D3992 head a six-locomotive line-up which includes four green liveried members of the same class which still sport the BR crest. The venue is the rear of Gloucester Horton Road depot on 14th October 1968 with long shadows signifying the approaching winter. Horton Road depot received seven of these Derby built shunters during the latter months of 1960. They were all new except for the fact that Tyseley depot had taken them in for acceptance trials before release to the depots; D3986, D3987, D3989, D3990, D3991, D3993 and D3994 all arrived between 8th October and 31st December. D3992 came a year later but others had been to Gloucester beforehand. D3360 was the first to be allocated on 1st November 1958 then, over the years up to 1968, came eight further examples which had variously been built at Darlington or Horwich.

Inverness based Sulzer Type 2 D5119 and sister 5130 (which we shall ignore from hereon) depart Aviemore on the evening of Monday 18th August 1969 with the 4.35 p.m. Inverness-Glasgow. By now both locomotives have the BR double-arrow motif but note that there are two different sizes involved and the locations are different too! All of the diesels working the lines north of Glasgow were equipped with three-part snowploughs which they carried year-round, the fleet at Inverness especially so. These two arrived at 60A in 1960, part of a sixteen strong batch supplied from Derby between May and September. They were later joined by the 'made-for-the-job' BRC&W Type 2s which were to be the backbone of locomotives hauled operations in the Highlands for many years. However, back to this pair of BR Sulzers: both survived to be renumbered under the TOPS scheme, becoming 24119 and 24130 respectively.

This is about as far north as we go in this album – the farthest northerly point in the series, and the country by rail. BR Sulzer Type 2 D5123, another of the intrepid band of Inverness Bo-Bos, stands awaiting departure from Thurso with the 5.20 p.m. to Inverness on Wednesday 4th September 1968. This example was also renumbered under TOPS and tidily became 24123. Like most of the Inverness batch, D5123 was transferred to Haymarket in exchange for further units of BRC&W Type 2s during the 1970s.

Passing the site of the former motive power depot, Gateshead based Sulzer Type 2 D5147 leaves Preston station behind and strides out for Blackpool in August 1967. It wasn't usual for 52A to have such clean looking locomotives available for traffic – a long drawn out trait from early BR steam days – but this Bo-Bo appears ex-works which would explain the anomaly! New to Gateshead on 17th December 1960, D5147 transferred to Holbeck on 25th November 1967. A cast 52A shedplate is still located on the left-hand connecting door of the front face next to the electrification warning flash but whoever painted the warning panel yellow painted the plate too.

Returning to the far north, we find BRC&W Type 2 D5325 stabled inside the station at Wick on 4th September 1968. Blue is the colour of the locomotive by this date, the large centrally positioned double-arrow unmistakable. The tablet-catching mechanism located in the No.2 end cab side sheet precludes the normal number position for that end of the locomotive but whereas at one time the main body panel immediately next to the drivers door would be used to display a number, only number has been applied, at this end. The other side of the locomotive would be similarly equipped with the tablet apparatus recessed in the No.1 end cab side and the number displayed on the No.2 cabside. Of course, some would say that having two numbers on the same side was extravagant whereas others might say having just one showing was somewhat parsimonious. Eventually BR adopted this single numbering scheme on a nation-wide basis and saved lots of money but made life difficult for trainspotters everywhere. This particular locomotive was not one of the first to work in these parts, and arrived in Inverness on 21st May 1960 along with sisters D5321 to D5337. They however, had been preceded by D5338 to D5346 which were transferred to 60A at the end of the previous February; the start of a long and mainly fruitful relationship had begun. At the same time three English Electric Type 1s – D8032 to D8034 – arrived in the capital of the Highlands to add their contribution towards the cessation of steam workings north of Perth. It was to take a while longer but the tools were now available; if only the weather holds out! It mustn't be forgotten that Brush Type 2 D5511 visited Inverness and environs during the summer of 1958 and spent two weeks in June, along with a week in July and another one in August showing its paces to the locals who were not impressed, apparently! 33

Back to the good ol' days when there was usually a choice of route! We're in Aviemore again but this time on 30th July 1964 with two departures for Inverness imminent. Both trains headed by BRC&W Type 2s (D5304 and D5327); one will travel via the main line, the other over the old route via Forres. The Cairngorms in the background sit beneath a brooding sky.

34

Still in BR green livery which is looking rather tired, BRC&W Type 2 D5398, departs Mallaig with the 12.15 p.m. service to Fort William on Friday 15th August 1969. The near 40-mile journey would be leisurely, picturesque and a treat and not to be undertaken by those in a hurry. D5398 started life at Cricklewood shed in north London during July 1962 and was one of the later examples of the Birmingham built Type 2s. Its passage to Scotland began in 1968 when it was allocated to Eastfield but just when the general lack of cleaning set in with these locomotives is unknown but D5398 appears to have a definite aura of neglect surrounding it. Even the 'M' (Midland Lines) allocation letters are still in situ long after it had been transferred to become part of the Nottingham Division in early 1968. Note the old engine shed, which was closed in June 1962, was still standing at this date and would remain so until the mid-80s' when a road scheme called for its demolition. D5398 did not outlive the engine shed and was a premature withdrawal in October 1975 (most of these locomotives worked into the mid to late 80s') although it was given the TOPS number 27039 in December 1973. It was still at Eastfield then, working the West Highland route as here. 35

The same train two days earlier, when it was being hauled by D5410, pauses at the delightful Glenfinnan station en route to Fort William. Again the green livery survives but its appearance is nothing short of atrocious. This was one of those which had three different TOPS numbers by dint of the fact that it was rebuilt at Derby with electric train heating and became Class 27/2. Its post-1973 numbers were 27123, 27205 and finally 27059. Withdrawn in July 1987, D5410 has been preserved in working order and has apparently been allocated a forth TOPS number – 89210. I wonder what its appearance is like these days?

And now for something completely different! This is what *D for Diesels* is all about. Diesel locomotives in Brunswick green livery with no yellow warning panels, and looking decidedly ex-works – we can dream. This is a section of Hornsey depot – 34B – before Finsbury Park depot – 34G – was commissioned in April 1960. The view was obtained from the footbridge which ran across the ECML from Hornsey station, across the goods and carriage lines and finally the northern entrance/exit to the shed to a point near the New river on the east side of the site. The three Brush 2s are D5605, D5593, and D5594, lined up on the fuelling racks provided as a temporary measure at this depot. All of the Type 2s are recently ex-works and have been through the acceptance trials meted out at Doncaster for all new diesel locomotives. The date is sometime just before 21st April 1960, the day 34G was officially opened for business. The three locomotives look rather comfortable in their surroundings but within a matter of weeks the role of Hornsey as a diesel depot will come to an end and Finsbury Park will come into its own taking on everything which the GN main line will require to move its trains. Just before the move to 34G from 34B, some 112 diesel locomotives were allocated to Hornsey shed and all of them would be transferred during the transition period lasting through late April 1960. The types and classes were broken down as follows: 6 EE Type 4s; 26 BRC&W Type 2s; 27 Brush Type 2s; 10 Baby Deltics; 11 NBL Type 2s; 13 EE Type 1s; 19 350 h.p. 0-6-0DE shunters! Quite an assortment and mostly acquired during a few short years before Finsbury Park was opened. About a third of their number would be transferred to Scotland prior to the short move across the main line but others were ready to take their place. Note the large fuel tanks erected on site to feed the diesel locomotives during their short sojourn at Hornsey. Finally, note that we have locomotives of the same class presenting their No.1 and No.2 end to the camera. It is from such a vantage point that we can see that only one works plate was fitted to these locomotives, on the secondmans side of the cab at the No.1 end as on D5605 and D5594.

The No.2 end of D5577 at Stratford in 1960! Allocated to Norwich depot from new on 31st December 1959 – the 32A shedplate is located on the cabside of No.1 end below the worksplate – D5577 moved on to March shed in late June 1962.

Brush D5678 on an e.c.s. working at King's Cross termini on the night of 6th February 1971. The empty stock is from an earlier arrival and is waiting for the right away to Holloway carriage sidings. Note the ghostly figure in the six-foot by the first carriage!

Now, pictures of Metro-Vick Co-Bos on Polmadie shed are fairly rare although we managed to present one in *DforD10* (page 20) which preceded this volume into publication. This is D5702 on No.14 road of Polmadie shed at sometime during August 1959, complete with the *CONDOR* headboard – now that is rare! The sunlight suggests that it is late evening and the noisy Type 2 is ticking over ready to move off shed in order to collect its train from Gushetfaulds for the overnight dash to London's Hendon. Another Metro-Vick would be leaving Hendon with the northbound working. Introduced on 16th March 1959, the overnight container service, running five nights a week, took approximately ten hours for the 400-mile, yard to yard journey (assuming the Co-Bos were behaving), the train weight was set at 550-tons, with all axles fitted with roller-bearings and every wagon air-braked. It was, in freight terms, the ideal train for the right motive power! As an aside, note how filthy those windows have become on the stores building alongside the locomotive; the windows on the Metro-Vick are positively sparkling. Ironically, the stores windows, which dated from about 1923, outlasted the locomotive!

An overhauled D5711 stands in the works yard at Crewe on 15th January 1967. Externally the locomotive looks entirely presentable but internally there were still many problems waiting to manifest themselves as components once again wore out or were loosened after the refurbishment in the shops. Multiply the problems by twenty and you have a large headache – each of the regions seemed to have their own although some to a lesser degree than others whilst some had NBL products and the Claytons! D5711 was condemned on 7th September 1968 along with the other remaining eleven members of the class. The LMR had had enough!

(*opposite*) We have entered a zone in the BR diesel locomotive numbering chronology which was inhabited by most of the less-than-welcome classes; we've just looked at a pair of Metro-Vicks and now we'll look at a couple of 'Baby Deltics' followed by the NBL Type 2 of the D61XX and D63XX classes – a real minefield but one which we, as enthusiasts, can relish because we didn't have to sort out the problems brought on by this lot. We start with an old friend, D5902 which is stabled at Finsbury Park depot on a very sunny but cold 23rd December 1961. This is the period whereby the troubles which had manifested over the previous couple of years were getting to such a pitch that drastic action was being taken by relegating the class to local trip working on freight or shunting. They simply could not be relied upon to whisk commuters in and out of King's Cross any more. D5902 may well have been given up by this date because it was taken over to High Meads at Stratford in the New Year for storage. Note how smart the Type 2 appears, although it may well have been ex-Doncaster Plant. For those with fond memories of other means of entertainment of that period, the roof prominent in the background belonged to the once famous Astoria – now a Pentecostal church – later renamed the Rainbow Theatre. (opposite, bottom) 1961 again and this EE Type 2 (these were of course the only Type 2 made by English Electric which had great success in all the other power ranges – 1, 3, 4, 5) is entrusted with a GN main line outer-suburban working . D5907 is at Welwyn Garden City and is showing, like No.2 the previous image, the original livery carried by the class which was altered when refurbished at Vulcan Foundry. Not only was the livery changed, the front end was also cosmetically altered, with the ladders removed, the connecting doors removed, the headcode discs discarded and a four character headcode panel fitted! With all the previous problems concerning the excessive weight and rectifying that, it was a foregone conclusion that the class were doomed – ten in the class therefore regarded as non-standard; problems from Day 1; ongoing service problems; rebuilding. They have been described as fascinating, interesting, breathtaking and, at the other end of the scale, ...! One, no two things regarding this class were set in concrete: they were not the favourites of BR, nor English Electric.

New to Kittybrewster depot from its arrival on 22nd March 1960, D6142 was loyal to that shed until it closed completely in August 1967 forcing the NBL-built Bo-Bo to 'move' to the former joint Caley/NBR shed at Ferryhill on the other side of the city. However, long before then, on 23rd August 1965 the Type 2 was active and was photographed at 61A wearing its original green livery with an added yellow warning panel (note the lower addition splash of yellow on the top half of the buffer shaft housings). The outer sections of the small 3-part snowplough are in situ too but the centre stub section is missing. At the No.1 end there appears to be no sign of any plough but it is summertime and we'll give the shed the benefit of the doubt. This locomotive was amongst the twenty NBL Type 2s which were delivered new to Kittybrewster in 1960. Most of them remained to the end – on paper – although quite a number had failed with distinction long beforehand and been put into store at various anonymous sheds and locations throughout north-east Scotland: Elgin, Keith, Inverurie, and Perth had many stored by the time the paper exercise of transfer from 61A to 61B was performed. Our subject was at that time actually stored unserviceable at Glasgow Eastfield and was condemned on the penultimate day of 1967. It was sold for scrap during the following April.

Some five feet shorter than their diesel-electric counterparts of D61XX Type 2 Bo-Bos, the Western Region diesel-hydraulic equivalent D63XX B-B Type 2 certainly appeared stubbier. However, these fifty-eight examples built for the WR were much more successful than their fifty-eight Scottish Region cousins. This clean-ish example, D6320, was stabled at Gloucester's Horton Road SP on 14th September 1968, on the site of the old steam shed where only the tracks and filled-in pits remained; the walls and roof were long gone. That the B-B was allocated to Bath Road in Bristol is undoubted, those two 82A shed plates at the end of the locomotive are there for all to see; was the same situation appertaining on the other side of D6320? Although the general appearance of tidy, there are a few oil stains/runs which might raise a few eyebrows amongst the fitting staff at its home shed. Whatever was the problem was soon sorted out and D6320 went on for a few more years until one repair too many forced it into storage in May 1971 under the new rules regarding diesel-hydraulics and the non-repair of! Another question, why fifty-eight of each??

In the good old days of April 1962 D6324 shunts the yard at Truro. This locomotive was delivered to the WR in June 1960 at Laira depot. Up to and including D6333 the class were fitted with the disc headcode system whilst D6334 onwards had the split four character headcode boxes. As certain of the lower numbered members went into works for overhaul they were retro-fitted with the headcode boxes; D6324 was one of those but later examples were given less prominent boxes than these examples which look like real bolt-on jobs with little thought as to the finish! Transferred to Bath Road on 15th January 1967, D6324 was also one of the early withdrawals; it was stored unserviceable in early 1968 and then, to de-clutter 82A, it was sent to Worcester – where it was stored from August 1968 – to be condemned on 14th September 1968. In the days before Swindon got back into the scrapping business, it was sold for scrap to Cashmores at Newport in May 1969.

It looks as though it has just been delivered! D6329 at Laira on Monday 27th June 1960 with very little evidence of work having been undertaken; this was apparently the last of the June deliveries which were all made, as usual, via Swindon for acceptance. Now this Type 2 had an interesting if somewhat short existence and was also one of the 1968 withdrawals. Transferred to Newton Abbot on 28th January 1961, D6329 returned to Laira five years later, to the day, only to whiz off to Bristol in January 1967. Newton Abbot called in September 1967 and on the 30th D6329 returned to Devon. However, just over a year later it was sent for store to Bath Road where it was withdrawn in November 1968. The same Newport scrapyard purchased the B-B in May 1969. It had a lot in common with D6324 but I'm not sure it received any headcode boxes. OAKLEY GRANGE looks on from across the shed yard whilst a couple of 'Warships' stake their claims on the south side of the shed site!

D6348 awaits a signal at Gloucester on the last day of July 1969 before heading off to the yards with freight from the Forest of Dean. Put into traffic at Laira on 23rd June 1962, this Type 2 lasted a while longer than the other examples so far reviewed. It left the West Country on 18th September 1965 having transferred from 83D to 83A on 12th June 1965. Its new home was to be Old Oak Common where it served the needs of Paddington for over two years until 24th February 1968 when it returned to Newton Abbot. Laira got it back at the end of June 68' but only for a matter of weeks because at the end of September it was off to the capital again. Periods in store, re-instatement's and a return to Plymouth took place over the ensuing years to withdrawal in July 1971. It was after one of the periods in store and re-instatement in June 1969 when it was captured on film for this less than glorious picture. Not to put too fine a point on it, D6348 was like the diesel locomotive equivalent of a stock-car, a very neglected and battered stock-car! After this outing, and many others, the B-B went back into store in February 1970 but was re-instated the following month – BR must have been desperately short of suitable motive power – to stay in traffic until the summer of 71'! Withdrawn in July 1971, it was taken to Swindon where it was broken up in May 1972.

Having left the twilight zone, we come back to reality where everything was sweetness and roses. Well you know what I mean. We have arrived at Hither Green depot in south-east London, a place which the BRC&W Type 3s made their home base from their introduction in December 1959. On Friday 8th April 1960 we are at the south end of the shed yard – the throat – to see brand new D6505 arriving on shed; delivery of this class was somewhat slow at first but it picked up to four a month by June 1960. Note that from the start these Bo-Bos were not fitted with connecting gangway doors, the SR seeing no reason why crews would need to transfer between locomotives. They didn't envisage using two locomotives in multiple either but other regions had that in mind for a certain service in particular which would see this class working as far north as York with a heavy cement train and on a daily basis; but that was in the future, nearly two years hence. In previous albums in this series we have shown these locomotives working the Cliffe-Uddingston bulk cement train on the ECML but it was nearly a year before their employment on the working that they began to visit certain depots on the ECML for crew training. Finsbury Park was naturally going to be the first due to its geographical position in relation to the working. D6504 spent a week there in February 1961 but that event was part of a much grander trial involving Derby's technical services section and trips between Edinburgh, London, Peterborough, and Derby; apparently nothing to do with bulk cement. Much later in the year D6559 was on loan to 34G from Bonfire Night for a week prior to going to New England for six weeks (every driver at NWE must have been trained up); D6556 joined it at NWE during that November (every driver was trained-up!). Further training sorties were carried out at 34G and 34E during 1962 and 1963 after the service had started and these involved Hither Green's Nos.D6517, D6541, and D6553.

Meanwhile, back on the Southern, the Type 3s started to stretch their wings from the south-eastern section to the South-western and everywhere in-between. D6506, showing the other end of this class, was photographed on Basingstoke shed when steam was still very much in charge of things on the old south-western main line. Provision for looking after diesel traction away from steam motive power was a problem encountered on every region of BR. Some had built dedicated new buildings for diesels, some had banished steam from old sheds and refurbished them (Hither Green for instance) whilst others tried to integrate the two which proved impossible. Money was in short supply on BR during the Modernisation period (and always it seems) so it was more a matter of make-do with whatever was to hand. On 27th August 1962 Hither Green gave up twelve of its Type 3s to Eastleigh shed so that further use of the type could be made in others areas of the region. Amongst that dozen was D6506 which appears to be without a shed plate but has the associated bolts in situ. Was it en route to 71A or just adding to its portfolio of 'sheds where I've stabled' after arrival in Hampshire. 49

We have looked at the EE Type 3 in various scenarios in this series but this is our first visit to see any of the class at Gloucester. Well, we have a treat with two of them stabled on Horton Road SP on separate days. (*above*) Tinsley based D6805 shows what a hefty pair of headcode boxes look like in this 19th April 1970 illustration. Late on for such things now, the 'D' prefixes are still in situ although Brush 1597 behind has lost its prefix. The bodywork of our subject looks a bit battered in the area above and to the right of the BR crest. Note that shed plates have gone but their painted equivalents live on – for now. A year earlier, (*below*) on 19th March 1969, Canton based D6969 was present to represent the four character headcode examples of the class. These were fitted from new to all of those EE Type 3s which went to the South Wales depots. The solid yellow warning panel now adorns the front of this Co-Co which is still in all-over green. Next step; all over blue, no prefix, TOPS number, and then .....!

Hymek D7007 departs from Gloucester (Central) and is passing Tramway Crossing with the 2.40 p.m. service from Gloucester to Swindon on 21st October 1961. New to Westbury shed on 7th October (on paper anyway), the B-B is still wearing that pristine just-out-of-the-box look and may well have been 'running-in' on Swindon acceptance trails. Note the Stanier '5' at the Eastgate platforms.

It seems possible that the Gloucester (Central)–Swindon 2.40 p.m. passenger service was a vehicle for newly delivered Hymeks to cut their teeth on. This undated view of D7000 shows it at Gloucester (Central) running round its train ready to work 2B79. Note the number of bodies in the cab! The previous image also had more than the normal complement of staff loitering within the cab indicating that locomotive trials or crew training was in force. D7000 certainly appears to be under the auspices of the testing department at Swindon. Officially, this locomotive was put into traffic at Bath Road shed on 25th May 1961 so this image could have been recorded at any time for a month either side of that date.

Straight to the start of the blue era now and we have D7052 parading that livery on 12th April 1968. The venue is Horton Road shed when most of the steam era infrastructure was still in place, but totally redundant. D7052 had started its career on 24th October 1962 at Bath Road shed but had latterly transferred to Cardiff Canton where it was based on this date. Even in the all-over blue with white window surrounds, these handsome locomotives still looked the business. Note that by now the cab doors had been fitted with a second lower handle.

BR Sulzer Type 2 D7501 stands at Sheffield (Midland) station on Sunday 26th April 1970. Put into traffic at Toton in October 1964, D7501 was soon in the thick of it earning a living from that once thriving East Midlands depot. Variously allocated to the Midlands Lines or Nottingham Division, D7501 ended up at Longsight (the retirement home for the EE Type 4 aka the 40s') and was withdrawn from there in September 1982 as 25151 having given eighteen years service to BR. Vic Berry took care of its remains but not at their yard in Leicester as for some reason it was cut up at Toton depot at the end of 1987.

EE Type 1 D8015 stands at Willesden shed on Sunday 15th March 1959. The design of this locomotive was set to become iconic; the locomotive itself was versatile, reliable, extremely useful, efficient, etc. One of the Pilot Scheme designs, it was to become the oldest type in use and is still performing somewhere in Britain even now! Allocated to Devons Road at this time, it would end up on the Eastern Region by the mid-60s' and would tread new ground for the class which was showing its paces to new audiences and winning friends every week. Note the wrong-facing BR crest and the Hornby-Dublo ladders (whatever happened to those?) located two-thirds of the way down the hood.

Now here is a sight which was not that common after the initial years of service – working hood first! D8024 has just come off the Scarborough line at York with a transfer freight for Dringhouses yard on 13th July 1971. Yes, that prefix is still in place – we are very selective you know!

Another of the early members of the class, but with a none-too early livery; this is D8030 at Stratford depot on 11th July 1970. The Bo-Bo is in full blue livery with full yellow ends, double-arrow BR symbol, but retaining the 'D' prefix. Once again, the accompanying Brush, 1778, has had its prefix painted out but it retains the two-tone green livery. Mix & match for modellers – brilliant!

Stabled amongst the skeletons of the steam age, D8192 and sister D8178 stand in the winter sunshine at Kirkby-in-Ashfield on Sunday 19th January 1969. On the left are the remains of the ex-Midland Railway coaling stage whilst towering over the pair is a BR-built ash plant which was actually a couple of years younger than what became Class 20! It took eleven years for all the members of the EE Type 1s to materialise on BR metals; not quite a record but nevertheless a formidable pedigree and one which in latter years was to prove their worth. Meanwhile, has anyone got a cleaning appliance? Locations such as Kirkby, Westhouses, Barrow Hill, Shirebrook, Worksop, and Colwick would each have between twenty and thirty diesel locomotives stabled at weekends. Throw in Toton, Tinsley and Wath and it was possible to 'cop' about a quarter of the BR main-line locomotive fleet which were mainly engaged during the week in moving one commodity – coal!

D8202 was one of the Yorkshire Engine Company built examples of the BTH Type 1 Bo-Bo. On 15th March 1959 it was photographed on Willesden depot with EE type 1 D8017 for company. Both Type 1 were allocated to Devons Road at the time and may well have been visiting the main shed 1A for various reasons. Both of these locomotives were transferred to Stratford when Devons Road was closed in February 1964.

Our first look at one of the 1967 EE Vulcan Foundry Type 1 builds, D8311 at York shed on 2nd July 1967. Straight out of the box this one, or so it appears, it was complete with blue livery and the double-arrow symbol, and four-character headcode at both ends. D8300 to D8328 represented the final version of this class which numbered two hundred and twenty-nine locomotives by the end of the build in February 1968. Now, this particular example was allocated to Thornaby when new, its official date for arrival on BR property was 28th April 1967, a Friday, which was usual for Vulcan Foundry deliveries. If Doncaster accepted D8311 it would have been in and out of the works testing regime within a couple of weeks maximum. However, the condition of the upper body, and more so the area below frame level, does not look like a locomotive which had been in traffic for seven weeks assuming the acceptance was for two also but even then road trials create dirt somewhere on the body. Have a look at the area around the exhaust which looks positively immaculate. What was wrong with this image? If you know, answers on a postcard, by e-mail or via the dog-and-bone to the usual. Looking at this Sunday photograph (compare with D8192), we can only assume that D8311 was on its initial delivery run to Thornaby. Not wishing to throw a spanner, etc., but York shed had a reputation for 'borrowing' new locomotives on delivery whenever they had a chance. Admitted, they had ten of these already so perhaps they had mistaken our subject for one of theirs but it still doesn't reveal the reason for such a clean locomotive. D8311 and her five Thornaby based sisters moved to Hull Dairycoates in March 1968, basically claiming new ground for the class.

Another one of the Pilot Scheme failures – the North British 800 h.p. Type 1 Bo-Bo – is represented by D8401 which has arrived at Doncaster for acceptance trails. The date is 13th July 1958, a Sunday when nothing much was happening at the Plant and enthusiasts were visiting to marvel at the latest diesel types sent by outside contractors – the Gresley Pacifics were secondary now!! The cab of our subject not only looks commodious from this aspect, it appears to have plenty of natural light considering it is located between the long and short hoods. Now have a look beneath the frame and marvel at the dirt-free environment under there. Different coloured paints indicate the various pipes, cables and air lines. D8401 has a tarpaulin secured over the front end air grills on top of the bonnet; I wonder why? On the right is another member of the class – D8400 – which also has a sheet over its front (No.1) end. D8400 had been completed during the previous October but NBL put the Bo-Bo through a thorough testing programme prior to releasing it to BR. It was only after the other nine members of the class were finally delivered that problems started to occur with the 16-cylinder Paxman engines. Mainly it was the cooling, or the lack of, which was creating allsorts of internal problems within the engine block. We all now know what happened to the class which had the manufacturers curse placed on them or was it those spoked wheels? Also in works that day, newly delivered, were D205, D206 and D5513 along with some Doncaster produced six-coupled shunting locomotives.

Clayton in trouble!? What's new! Blue liveried D8503 stands at Motherwell on 9th September 1971 with engine compartment doors open, and fluids dripping over the running plate. Is that smoke staining on the inside of the doors? Is another Type 1 finished? The answer to the last question is yes which indicates that the previous question could be answered with a yes too. This particular Clayton had already been stored and re-instated twice during its short life but this time there would be no comeback. A one-way trip to Glasgow works was forthcoming and after a period of outside storage, the inevitable took place in June 1972. The EE Type 3, 6856 looks like the rescue vehicle assuming the Clayton couldn't make its own way back to the depot.

D8549 in basically better days – if there were any – at Polmadie depot at 1515 hours on Friday 23rd October 1964! Green livery was still in vogue but cleaning wasn't, especially in Glasgow but the windows of the Clayton look commendably clean – you have to be positive about something!

One of the Rolls-Royce powered Claytons, D8587 stables at Millerhill yard on 10th August 1969. Sister D8586, which was never far away, is buffered up. Both of these locomotives spent the whole of their lives allocated to Haymarket depot where comparisons could be continually made with the Paxman engined members of the class allocated to 64B. The neglect is showing on the paintwork of D8687 but nothing will be done to make it right; the Scottish Region had just about given up trying to make something from this class. It was never going to work. It was funny in some ways but the Scottish Region had been dealt a couple of particularly bad hands but they had been represented by two separate players who didn't communicate with each other, play as a team, or offer any mutual assistance. The former Caledonian lines had the Claytons whilst the former North British lines had the NBL D6100 Type 2s. Rarely did the two meet and when they did, as at Haymarket for instance, only one of the troubled classes was present. I suppose a shed foreman with a shed full of Claytons and D61XXs together might in the end leave the job prematurely but that event never happened and they managed to keep the two rogues apart, in the main.

After another small diversion into the doldrums, we come out into the blazing sunshine of a December day in 1961. Finsbury Park is the venue and one of their illustrious 'Deltic' steeds is the subject. We have featured D9001 ST PADDY before, a few times but never at Finsbury Park. Earlier we mentioned extravagance and parsimony with worksplates, etc. Well, for the accountants amongst you, this lot had four works plates, four BR crests (all correct facing), four sets of numbers, and two nameplates – each! Next came the shedplates but they were fitted by the individual sheds and different ideas abounded. Can you spot the 34G plate here?

A little later in the decade, on Saturday afternoon 14th June 1969, D9003 MELD comes storming into Peterborough with 1E07, a Waverley–King's Cross express. By now blue livery with full yellow ends and the double-arrow motif had become the order-of-the-day for the twenty-two chosen ones. The next change would be the introduction of white paint around the cab windows.

D9014 THE DUKE OF WELLINGTON'S REGIMENT makes its way out of Heaton carriage sidings with stock for a special working (note the all LMS origin) from Newcastle to King's Cross on 14th June 1967. Although looking a bit shabby – it was a Gateshead steed – D9014 has just been given full yellow ends on one of its frequent visits to Doncaster.

Going back just five years to Monday 18th June 1962 and we find D9020 NIMBUS wowing the crowds of assembled BR personnel gathered to see-off *THE FLYING SCOTSMAN* on its northbound centenary run. The immaculate 'Deltic' has been given a small yellow warning panel which does not detract. D9020 and fellow Finsbury Park resident D9001 had the dubious distinction of being the first of the class to be withdrawn. But that is some albums away yet so let's enjoy sights like this and the next one which features a new 'Deltic' to the series.

The last of the class gets to Doncaster at last! D9021 was destined to be allocated to Haymarket depot once the acceptance trials had been completed but that was some days off yet. The date is 29th April 1962, a Sunday and D9021 had arrived in south Yorkshire during the previous week after spending a week or so in Manchester conducting trials with A.C. electric locomotives on the Styal line. During its enforced diversion the Type 5 stabled each night in the sidings at Mauldeth Road station, a regular location for stock and locomotives under testing along the 25kV stretch of railway. Note that the usual immaculate aura which accompanied these locomotives on their one day delivery run from Newton-le-Willows is gone and a coat of road dirt has replaced the ex-works sheen. The fuel tanks have been shaken about somewhat and many leaks have shown themselves. The tests on the suburban route entailed speed trials up to and over 100 m.p.h. with sudden braking and rapid acceleration being parts of the routine. Rumours at the time said it was electric v diesel but it wasn't that simple apparently. Somewhere there exists results and notes concerning those short time tests; if anyone has a copy, the staff at Book Law would like to peruse the same. In anticipation, thanks! Finally, has anyone noticed that four BR crests are no longer required – not with the new larger super-duper crest set in the centre of the body. Now, about that nameplate!

I don't know how many 0-6-0s were constructed at Swindon over the lifetime of those workshops but this diesel-hydraulic was the culmination of all of those which had gone before. Whereas the steam predecessors had each gone onto work for at least thirty years apiece, and some of the diesel-mechanical examples had put in twenty or so years, this class which were constructed during 1964/65 and were the last of the line, managed less than ten years service before withdrawal. What brought about their construction is unknown – politics, stupidity, blind optimism, desperation – and we probably never will know but fifty-six of them were eventually built to work pick-up goods, trip working and even shunting. Here class leader D9500 – allocated to Bath Road at the time – is traversing the rails at Gloucester (Eastgate) as though going out for a morning run on 24th February 1967. It may well have been making its way to the junction to reverse so that it could head off to Cardiff at a leisurely pace – it transferred to Canton on 20th May 1967 – without having to use the tunnel. Put into store in December 1967, it was re-instated at the end of February 1968 but was then withdrawn in April 1969. Today it is preserved, one of twenty of the class which miraculously survived into preservation.

Immaculate in every way! Not yet delivered D9508 stands ready for action at Swindon on Sunday 6th September 1964. Still Swindon wouldn't comply with BR number font guidelines, these were apparently painted-on, note also the use of the coaching stock version of the BR crest. One thing which did go in Swindon's favour was the use of the two door handle location the lower one nicely recessed so as not to impede egress. According to the record, D9508 went to Canton depot the very next day to start a short relationship which ended in May 1965 when Landore beckoned. Periods in store saw the 0-6-0DH do little in the way of work and it was withdrawn on 5th October 1968; the majority of the class had been withdrawn during the previous April. Purchased by the National Coal Board for goodness knows how much! D9508 was towed up to Ashington for a worthwhile career working the rail system associated with the collieries in that part of Northumberland. It was cut up in January 1984 so lets say somebody got nearly twenty years work out of the six-coupled diesel.   71

Here is a sight to make you shudder especially if you ever witnessed the passing of condemned steam locomotives through Gloucester to the scrapyards of South Wales during the great steam cull. This line-up of redundant Type 1 0-6-0DH – Nos.D9527 (which has had a hefty clout), D9502, D9514, and D9518 – at Horton Road depot Gloucester on 4th July 1969 were in fact going in the opposite direction to their steam cousins. The four had all been allocated to Cardiff Canton during their working days with BR and had all been withdrawn in April 1969 – amongst the last ten to go. All were en-route to Hull Dairycoates for storage prior to being sold. Now, two of them ended up in preservation and two went into industry and were eventually broken up in January 1984 and December 1985 respectively (there's a clue already). No it's not a new competition whereby you fill in the gaps and we give out the prizes but this teaser is designed to involve you a bit more so that you can say what went where? Answers, if you don't already know, in *DforD11*!